WHY STEPHEN F. AUSTIN MATTERS TO TEXAS

By Lynn Peppas

I0792483

Published in 2014 by The Rosen Publishing Group, Inc.
29 East 21st Street, New York, NY 10010

Copyright © 2014 by Digital Discovery Publishing

All rights reserved. No part of this book may be reproduced in any form without permission in writing from the publisher, except by a reviewer.

First Edition

Developed, written, and produced by Digital Discovery Publishing
Editors: Molly Aloian, Wendy Scavuzzo
Design & Production: Katherine Berti
Curriculum & content coorindator: Reagan Miller
Photo research: Crystal Sikkens, Allison Napier
Proofreader: Sarah Cairns
Special Thanks: Bryan McAuley, Site Manager, San Felipe de Austin State Historic Site

Photo Credits: Brazoria County Historical Museum: 10 (bottom)
Digital Discovery Publishing: 1, 5, 6, 13, 16 (left)
Dolph Briscoe Center for American History, Austin, Texas: 22, 25
General Land Office, Austin, Texas: 16 (right)
The Granger Collection, NYC: 19
Kentucky Museum, Western Kentucky University, Bowling Green: 9 (top right)
Library of Congress: 7, 12
Missouri History Museum, St. Louis: 9 (top)
North Wind Picture Archives: 8, 12
Rugeley-Moore Collection, Richmond, Texas: 29 (top)
The San Jacinto Museum of History, Houston: 4, 20
Shutterstock: 5, 6
Texas State Library & Archives: cover, 14 (top)
University of Texas at San Antonio Libraries Special Collections: 10 (top)
Wikimedia Commons: cover, 6 (top), 11, 15, 26, 29 (bottom)

All websites were live and accurate at the time of printing.

Library of Congress Cataloging-in-Publication Data

Peppas, Lynn.
Why Stephen F. Austin matters to Texas / by Lynn Peppas.
p. cm. – (Texas perspectives)
Includes index.
ISBN 978-1-4777-0914-6 (library binding) – ISBN 978-1-4777-0934-4 (pbk.) – ISBN 978-1-4777-0935-1 (6-pack)
1. Austin, Stephen F. (Stephen Fuller), 1793-1836 – Juvenile literature. 2. Pioneers – Texas – Biography – Juvenile literature. 3. Frontier and pioneer life –Texas – Juvenile literature. 4. Texas - History – Revolution, 1835-1836 – Juvenile literature. 5. Texas – History – To 1846 – Juvenile literature. I. Peppas, Lynn. II. Title.
F389.A942 P47 2013
976.4'05–dc23

Manufactured in the United States of America

CPSIA Compliance Information: Batch W13PK: For Further Information contact Rosen Publishing, New York, New York at 1-800-237-9932

CONTENTS

1 A FATHER'S DREAM

In June 1821, Stephen Austin's mother, Maria, wrote her son a letter saying she was "alarmed" about his father's health. Stephen's father, Moses, had recently come home to Missouri from a business trip in Texas. Moses had succeeded in his business in Texas, but the journey home had been hard and he was very ill.

Stephen's mother wrote to him on June 8, 1821:

"He called me to his bed side and with much distress and difficulty of speech. He begged me to tell you to take his place and...go on with the business in the same way he would have done had not sickness and... perhaps death, prevented him..."

Moses Austin was given approval to settle 300 Anglo-American families on 200,000 acres (80,937 ha) of land in Texas. The task was taken over by his son Stephen Austin (left) when Moses died.

Moses died just two days after Maria wrote the letter. He did not leave his family any money. The only thing Moses passed on to his 27-year-old son, Stephen, was his dream of settling the first Anglo Americans in the Spanish-owned **province** of Texas.

Stephen decided to fulfill his father's dream. He continued with Moses's plan and led the first Anglo-American families into the unknown wilderness of Texas.

Texas Perspective

Stephen Austin became the first Anglo-American **empresario** in Texas.

STEPHEN AUSTIN'S TEXAS

2 GROWING UP

Stephen Fuller Austin was born on November 3, 1793, in Austinville, Virginia. Stephen had a sister, Emily, who was born in 1795. A brother, James Elijah Brown Austin, nicknamed "Brown," was born in 1803.

When Stephen was five years old, the Austin family moved to what is now Missouri to start a lead-mining business. Mine à Breton was an untouched wilderness. Only a few hundred people lived nearby, including French, Spanish, Anglo Americans, and African Americans. Young Stephen often played with nearby Indian and African-American children.

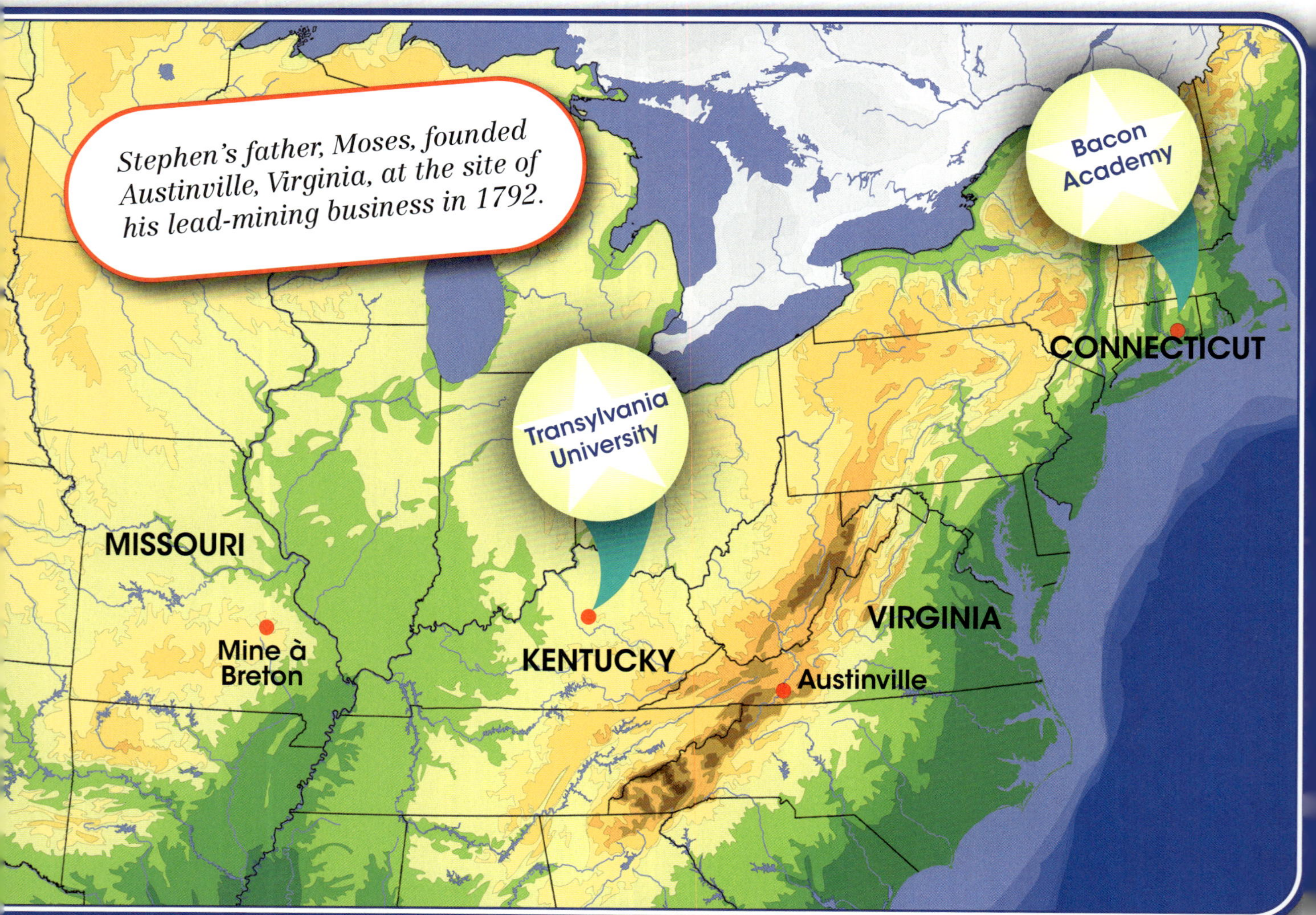

Moses Austin established a settlement west of the Mississippi River at Mine à Breton. This area is now Potosi, Missouri.

SCHOOL DAYS

Stephen did not begin his formal education until he was 11 years old. In 1804, his family sent him to Connecticut to attend a school called Bacon Academy. Life at Bacon Academy was a completely new experience for Stephen. He studied subjects such as English, grammar, mathematics, and geography. Moses Austin wanted Stephen's education to help him become a businessman.

In 1809, Stephen began to study at Transylvania University in Lexington, Kentucky, but he did not graduate. When the family's lead mine ran into financial trouble, Moses pulled his son out of school. In April 1810 Stephen began to help his father at the mine.

Stephen went to Bacon Academy for three years. The school had very strict rules.

▲ *Stephen served as quartermaster for the soldiers on horseback during the War of 1812.*

WAR OF 1812

Stephen worked at the family mine until May 1813. At that time, the United States was at war with the British in the **War of 1812**. Stephen volunteered for the Americans and was put in charge of supplies for his **regiment**. Stephen learned how to supply hundreds of people with food, navigate through remote wilderness areas, and negotiate with Indians.

FAMILY DEBT

Stephen returned home from the war in October 1813. His family had fallen further into **debt** because of the war. Stephen was a loyal son who was not afraid of hard work. He wanted to help get his family out of debt. Over the next few years, Stephen took on many jobs that taught him important life lessons. Many of these experiences prepared Stephen for his later role of empresario in Texas.

From a letter Stephen wrote to his brother-in-law, James Bryan, in December 1818:

> *"When the day arrives that the whole family are out of debt I mean to [celebrate] it as my wedding day—which will never come [until] then."*

*In 1815, at age 22, Stephen won an election to Missouri's **legislature**. Stephen met in this house to work on laws to improve the lives of people in Missouri.*

Joseph Hawkins supported Stephen for many years. Hawkins let Stephen live in his home and use his books so he could study and become a lawyer, too.

JOSEPH H. HAWKINS

In late 1820, Stephen moved to New Orleans to find work. At that time, jobs were hard to find anywhere. In New Orleans, Stephen met a successful lawyer named Joseph H. Hawkins who helped him during this difficult time. Hawkins became one of Stephen's best friends.

Stephen showed his appreciation for Hawkins's friendship in this letter to his mother on January 20, 1821:

"...I came here with a hope of getting employ; I offered to hire myself out as clerk, as an overseer, or anything else, but business is too dull here to get into business....In this state of things it was my good fortune to get acquainted with Joseph H. Hawkins...who gave me employ in an office....He has kindly advanced me money enough to purchase a few groceries for you and sister..."

3 TEXAS BOUND

▲ *Baron de Bastrop continued to help Stephen after Moses's death.*

While Stephen was in New Orleans, Moses Austin went to Texas, which was part of Mexico. He asked the Spanish governor for permission to settle Anglo Americans in Texas. It did not go well, though. Moses was ordered to leave Texas and never return.

BARON DE BASTROP

Moses's luck changed when he met a man called the Baron de Bastrop. The Baron was an influential man and spoke to the governor on Moses's behalf. A few days later, the governor accepted Moses's application to settle Anglo Americans in Texas.

Moses left Texas to return to the United States. The weather was cold and the journey was difficult. When Moses finally arrived home, he was sick. Despite his illness, Moses continued to ask Stephen to "put aside his doubts," and join him in settling Texas.

MOSES AUSTIN

▲ *Moses Austin was born on October 4, 1761. He is known as the father of the lead mining industry in the United States.*

Moses Austin was an American mining industry **pioneer**. Although he was financially successful for many years, he eventually lost his fortune. However, he was not the type of person to give up easily. He hoped to regain the family fortune by starting the first American **colony** in the Spanish province of Texas. In May 1821, Moses was the first American to get permission from the Spanish government to establish a colony in Texas. Unfortunately, Moses died the next month. It was up to his son, Stephen, to make the dream of settling Americans in Texas a reality.

CARRYING ON

Moses wrote to Joseph Hawkins and asked him to invest money in his project to colonize Texas. Hawkins thought it was a good idea and agreed to give money to help support the project. Hawkins convinced Stephen to become more interested in it, too. Stephen traveled to Texas with a group of Spanish officials. Before they left, Stephen mailed out an **advertisement** to be printed in newspapers. He was looking for Anglo Americans interested in moving to Texas. Stephen learned of his father's death during his journey but continued on. He knew it was what Moses would have wanted him to do.

Moses Austin was buried in Missouri. Many people want to move his body so he can be laid to rest in Texas, the place where his dream was accomplished.

FIRST IMPRESSIONS

During his travels, Stephen was amazed at the many kinds of wildlife in Texas. The foods the group ate included deer, buffalo, and honey. Stephen described finding "grapes in immense quantities on low vines." He came across many creeks, springs, and rivers that he reported as clear and "sufficiently large for mills." The group also met with Indians during the trip.

This is an excerpt from a journal that Stephen kept as he traveled through Texas on August 10, 1821:

"...came on to the Guadalupe River, country [was] the most beautiful I ever saw, rolling prairies soil very black and deep..."

US EXPANSIONISM

In the early 1800s, many Americans believed that their country's boundary should expand westward to the Pacific Ocean. At that time, Spain and France owned much of that territory. The United States bought a large piece of land from France in 1803 for about $15 million. That deal was called the Louisiana Purchase. It included modern-day states such as Arkansas, Missouri, Iowa, Oklahoma, Kansas, and Nebraska, and parts of many others. In 1820, the American government wanted farmers to pay for and settle the land the country had purchased. Many farmers could not afford to buy American land, though. These farmers instead looked to Texas, which was still owned by Spain, because the land there was free. The Spanish government said that colonists who moved to Texas didn't have to pay them any tax for the first four years. However, the colonists had to become Mexican citizens, follow the Roman Catholic religion, and live under Mexican laws.

The Louisiana Purchase included all or part of 15 modern states and land that would later become part of Canada.

Stephen sketched this map of Texas in 1822.

The Brazos River is the longest river in Texas. It was an important source of water for Stephen's colonists as they established their new rural community.

PICKING A SITE

When Stephen returned from Texas, he wrote to the Mexican government that he had chosen lands between the Brazos and San Jacinto rivers. It was some of the best farmland in the area. Stephen and Governor Antonio Martínez decided that each farming family would be given about 177 acres (72 ha) of farmland. Those who raised livestock would be given 4,428 acres (1,792 ha).

OFF TO TEXAS

Stephen moved to Texas in December 1821. When he arrived at the mouth of the Colorado River, the men and farming supplies were nowhere to be found. He searched for weeks but never found them. He was counting on the supplies and men aboard the ship to start the colony. Without them, starting out would be much harder for the 100 colonists who had recently arrived on land near the Colorado River. Another 50 colonists had settled on the Brazos River.

This large cathedral is in Mexico City.

OFF TO MEXICO

By March 1822, the colonists began to clear the land and plant corn. Stephen traveled to San Antonio to report to Governor Martínez, but he discovered bad news. Mexico had declared independence the year before, so the previous agreements between Stephen and the Spanish government in Mexico were in question. The governor suggested that Stephen go to Mexico City to talk to the newly formed Mexican government. In mid-March, Stephen set out on horseback toward Mexico City.

MEXICAN WAR OF INDEPENDENCE

Acta de independencia del Imperio Mexicano, pronunciada por su Junta Soberana, congregada en la Capital de él en 28 de Setiembre de 1821.

La Nación Mexicana que, por trescientos años, ni ha tenido voluntad propia, ni libre el uso de la voz, sale hoy de la opresion en que ha vivido.

Los heroicos esfuerzos de sus hijos han sido coronados, y está consumada la empresa, eternamente memorable, ...

Spanish explorers first arrived in Mexico in the 1500s. Spain claimed the land and called it New Spain. Many years later, the people of Mexico wanted to govern themselves and be independent from Spain. The Mexican War of Independence began in 1810. The Mexican people and the Spanish **loyalists** fought for 11 years. Independence for Mexico was finally achieved in 1821.

In 1821, the Treaty of Córdoba promised Mexican independence. At first, the new Mexican government would not honor previous land grants. This put Stephen's new colony in danger.

IN MEXICO CITY

Stephen arrived in Mexico City at the end of April. He soon learned that the Mexican government was in a constant state of confusion. Then General Agustín de Iturbide took power in Mexico in May 1822. Stephen felt hopeful that the new government would finally organize so he could secure his **petition** for a colony in Texas. He wrote a letter to Iturbide in which he promised to pledge his oath of allegiance to Mexico. He also taught himself to speak and write the Spanish language.

It took the Mexican government a long time to make its colonization laws. Iturbide was overthrown and another government was set up. When the colonization laws were finally announced on April 11, 1823, the land grants continued as before. As before, the settlers had to become Mexican citizens and practice the Roman Catholic religion.

EMPRESARIO, AT LAST

Stephen finally rode out of Mexico City on April 18, 1823, as Texas's first Anglo-American empresario. It had taken more than a year, but his colony had finally been approved.

General Iturbide, also known as Agustín I, was killed just two years after he crowned himself emperor of Mexico.

4 LIFE IN THE COLONY

Stephen was eager to get back to his new colony in Texas. He returned in August 1823 with the Baron de Bastrop. As empresario, Stephen was responsible for bringing new settlers into his colony, distributing their land accurately, and maintaining law and order. He would also oversee the building of roads, schools, and businesses to support the colony. Stephen's job also included acting as a go-between for the colonists and the Mexican government on issues that affected the colony.

SAN FELIPE DE AUSTIN

Stephen had to establish a capital for the colony. In the summer of 1823, he chose the location of the town of San Felipe de Austin. It was on the Brazos River about 60 miles (97 km) away from the Gulf of Mexico. He also started what came to be known as the Texas Rangers—men who were hired to protect the settlers.

▲ *This is a plan of the town of San Felipe de Austin.*

This replica log cabin stands at San Felipe de Austin State Historic Site today.

THE OLD THREE HUNDRED

Stephen spent all of his time working to make the colony a better place. He could not do all the work himself, though. He needed help to organize his office and to keep careful track of land grants and other records. He hired Samuel May Williams as his secretary. Baron de Bastrop was in charge of issuing proper land titles for the colonists.

By late 1824, Stephen had fulfilled his first empresario contract and brought 300 Anglo-American families to settle in his colony. These first settlers are known as the Old Three Hundred.

Texas Perspective

Stephen Austin settled more than 1,200 families in Texas between 1821 and 1836.

The first families Stephen granted land to had to be honest and hardworking to make the colony a success.

INDIANS IN TEXAS

There were many groups of Indians, such as the Karankawa and Tonkawa, living in Texas when Stephen and the colonists arrived. The Indians had been hunting and fishing on these lands for hundreds of years. Stephen tried to keep the peace between the Indians and the colonists by bringing the Indians gifts such as farming tools and seeds. The Indians preferred their traditional ways of life, though, and did not want to live like the American settlers.

In 1825, the Mexican military commander ordered Stephen to declare war against the Waco Indians. Stephen wrote to the Mexican officials and told them that a war might cause all the nearby Indians to unite and fight against the American colonists. A peace treaty was signed instead.

Stephen's letter to Mexican officials on September 28, 1825, shows he preferred peace to war:

"...is there not some danger that all the Indians in the province may be induced to unite against the American settlements? If we destroy the Waco villages will not the other tribes consider it as a warning of the fate that must in the end befall them if the American settlements progress?"

COAHUILA AND TEXAS

In April 1824, the Mexican government formed a new constitution that joined two of its provinces together. The new area was called Coahuila and Texas. In 1825, Mexico passed a law that encouraged more colonists to settle in the new province. In 1825, 1827, and 1828, Stephen got permission to settle more families in Texas. Some of the colonists were unhappy with the Mexican government, though. They wanted to break away and become an independent nation. That created new problems for Stephen.

THE FREDONIAN REBELLION

In 1824, an empresario named Haden Edwards settled a colony near Stephen's. Edwards was not a good empresario. He charged his colonists high fees and did not give them proper land deeds. Mexican leaders started to hear complaints about Haden Edwards and his brother Benjamin. In June 1826, the Mexican president canceled the brothers' contract and tried to force them out of Mexico.

In November, Benjamin Edwards and 35 other armed men rode into Nacogdoches, Texas, and arrested local officials there. Later, the group declared their independence from Mexico and called their new nation the Republic of Fredonia. They claimed Texas as their own. The Edwards brothers also asked other empresarios and their colonists to join in the fight, but most refused.

Stephen formed a small force to help the Mexican army stop the rebellion.

COLONIAL LOYALTY?

Mexican troops marched against the Edwards brothers' force in January 1827. The Edwards brothers escaped and, by the end of January, the rebellion was over. Stephen argued that the lack of support from the colonists proved their loyalty to the government of Mexico. However, Mexican government officials were certain that another rebellion would soon break out among the American settlers and the Indians.

During its early years, the town had three mercantile stores, two taverns, one hotel, one blacksmith shop, and about 40 to 50 log cabin homes.

GROWTH OF THE COLONY

By 1828, Stephen's town was named San Felipe de Austin, and it had a **population** of about 200 residents. The majority of people who lived there were Anglo-American men. San Felipe grew steadily. San Felipe's first school was established by Thomas Pilgrim. Forty students, most of whom were boys, attended the school in 1829. Three more schools were founded by the end of 1830. A lumber and grain mill was also established around 1830.

Many came to the colony to grow crops or raise livestock. A few families brought slaves to the colony to help with the farming. The settlers grew crops such as cotton, sugar, corn, and potatoes. By 1835 the town had added a land office and post office. The population had grown to about 600 residents, and many more lived in the outskirts.

FAMILY LOSS

In August 1829, Stephen's brother, Brown, sailed to New Orleans on a business trip. He caught yellow fever there and died within days. Stephen was very close to his brother. The news of Brown's death affected him so much that he became ill and was bedridden for almost a month.

Stephen wrote to his cousin, Henry Austin:

> ***"I have just returned (so to speak) from the brink of the grave and I have received a terrible blow in the death of my only brother, companion in so much hardship...that we passed through together in this wilderness..."***

SURROUNDED BY FAMILY

After the death of his brother, Stephen needed his family with him more than ever. Stephen's sister, Emily, her husband, James Perry, and their family made the move to Texas in 1831. The arrival of Stephen's cousin Mary Austin Holley also brightened his spirits. Mary shared Stephen's love for books and music. The two spent a lot of time together, and her company made Stephen extremely happy.

Stephen wrote about his feelings of happiness to Mary in December, 1831:

> ***"...how shall I ever thank you for venturing into this wilderness—how [shall I] express the happiness of the ten days visit...[?]"***

UNREST GROWS

During this time, the Mexican government feared a **revolution** in Texas. Mexican officials sent General Manuel de Mier y Terán to investigate the Anglo-American settlements. Even though Mier y Terán had great respect for Stephen, he warned his government that the Anglo-American settlers could begin a revolution soon.

A new Mexican government passed The Law of April 6, 1830 to stop Anglo Americans from **immigrating** to Texas, raise tariffs on imported goods, and increase the number of soldiers in the area. Many Mexican citizens were forced to move to Texas. By the end of 1832, there were five times more Anglo Americans living in Texas than Mexicans.

Anglo-American colonists grew increasingly angry with the Mexican government and its new laws. Anglo Americans began to clash with Mexican authorities and refused to pay taxes. Mexican government officials felt that a revolution was close.

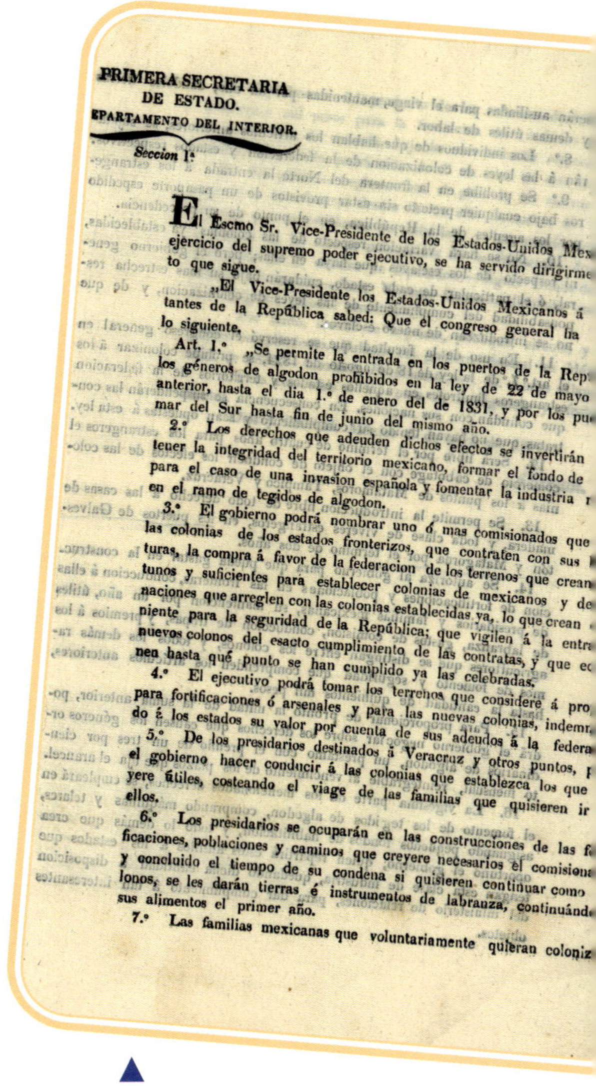

PRIMERA SECRETARIA
DE ESTADO.
EPARTAMENTO DEL INTERIOR.
Seccion 1ª

El Escmo Sr. Vice-Presidente de los Estados-Unidos Mex
ejercicio del supremo poder ejecutivo, se ha servido dirigirme
to que sigue.

„El Vice-Presidente los Estados-Unidos Mexicanos á
tantes de la República sabed: Que el congreso general ha
lo siguiente.

Art. 1.° „Se permite la entrada en los puertos de la Rep
los géneros de algodon prohibidos en la ley de 22 de mayo
anterior, hasta el dia 1.° de enero del de 1831, y por los pu
mar del Sur hasta fin de junio del mismo año.

2.° Los derechos que adeuden dichos efectos se invertirán
tener la integridad del territorio mexicano, formar el fondo de
para el caso de una invasion española y fomentar la industria
en el ramo de tegidos de algodon.

3.° El gobierno podrá nombrar uno ó mas comisionados que
las colonias de los estados fronterizos, que contraten con sus
turas, la compra á favor de la federacion de los terrenos que crean
tunos y suficientes para establecer colonias de mexicanos y de
naciones que arreglen con las colonias establecidas ya, lo que crean
niente para la seguridad de la República; que vigilen á la entr
nuevos colonos del esacto cumplimiento de las contratas, y que ec
nen hasta qué punto se han cumplido ya las celebradas.

4.° El ejecutivo podrá tomar los terrenos que considere á pro
para fortificaciones ó arsenales y para las nuevas colonias, indemn
do á los estados su valor por cuenta de sus adeudos á la federa

5.° De los presidarios destinados á Veracruz y otros puntos,
el gobierno hacer conducir á las colonias que establezca los que
yere útiles, costeando el viage de las familias que quisieren ir
ellos.

6.° Los presidarios se ocuparán en las construcciones de las f
ficaciones, poblaciones y caminos que creyere necesarios el comision
y concluido el tiempo de su condena si quisieren continuar como
lonos, se les darán tierras é instrumentos de labranza, continuánd
sus alimentos el primer año.

7.° Las familias mexicanas que voluntariamente quieran coloniz

The law of April 6, 1830 (above), tried to encourage Mexican citizens to move to Texas by offering them good land and money to settle.

SLAVERY IN TEXAS

Slavery was illegal in Mexico, but it was legal in many parts of the United States until 1865. Stephen feared that the Mexican government would ban slavery in its state of Coahuila and Texas. Stephen fought against the abolition of slavery because he knew it would anger many of the Anglo-American colonists in Texas who owned slaves.

Texas Perspective

Stephen Austin was unwilling to recommend war with Mexico as long as peace was still possible.

A PETITION

The Mexican government was overthrown once again in 1833. Antonio López de Santa Anna was elected as the Mexican president. **Delegates** from Texas presented a petition to Santa Anna and the newly formed Mexican government. The petition asked the Mexican government to separate Texas from Coahuila so Texas could become its own state. The delegates also created their own constitution for a new state of Texas. They gave the petition to Stephen to present to the government in Mexico City. Stephen delivered the proposed constitution in July. He knew that war could break out if Mexico did not grant his colonists' petitions.

In a letter to Henry Austin, on April 19, 1833, Stephen said:

"This is my last effort to serve Texas, if I succeed I shall be happy, and will try to enjoy some comfort in future... If however I fail, and war is the result, I will take a hand in that, and enter the ranks as a soldier of Texas[.]"

SAM HOUSTON

Sam Houston moved to Texas in 1832. He played a leading role in the growth of Texas for more than 25 years. During the Texas Revolution, Houston led the Texas army and won the Battle of San Jacinto, which gave Texas its independence from Mexico. Houston was elected the first president of the Republic of Texas and then worked hard to bring Texas into the United States union.

Sam Houston was first elected president of Texas from 1836 to 1838. He defeated Stephen Austin for the job.

DELAYS IN MEXICO

The journey to Mexico City was extremely long and difficult. Stephen arrived on July 18 to find an outbreak of cholera in the city. The outbreak killed thousands in Mexico City, and the Mexican government offices closed before they had considered the petition from Texas.

When the Mexican congress reopened in September, they reversed the law that had banned new Anglo-American settlers from coming to Texas. Stephen met with President Santa Anna about the issue of separate statehood for Texas, but no decisions were made by the time Stephen left Mexico City in December. He felt that statehood was still possible, but he expected it would take some time.

PEACE OR WAR?

Back in Texas, colonists had formed two groups, called the Peace Party and the War Party. Most of the men in the War Party were younger, unmarried, and had recently moved to Texas. They wanted to revolt. The men in the Peace Party were mostly older, married colonists who had lived in Texas for a longer time. They wanted to stay loyal to Mexico. Many more settlers flocked to Texas after the law that banned American immigration had been reversed. In 1835, about 30,000 Anglo Americans lived in Texas.

Antonio López de Santa Anna played a key role in the Mexican revolution. He revoked the Mexican Constitution of 1824, which angered the people of Texas and sparked the revolution.

IMPRISONED!

Stephen did not make it back to Texas. Instead, he was arrested in Saltillo on January 2, 1834. A Mexican official in San Antonio received a letter from Stephen during his stay in Mexico City. In the letter, Stephen suggested that Texans form their own government before getting approval from President Santa Anna. Government officials viewed his letter as proof that Stephen was trying to start a revolution. He was taken to Mexico City and jailed.

At first, Stephen was kept in a small prison cell that had no windows and very little light. He was kept in solitary confinement, which meant he had no contact with others for three months. Later, he was moved to other prisons with less harsh conditions. On December 25, 1834, Stephen was finally released. He had been in jail for almost one year. He was free but could not leave Mexico City.

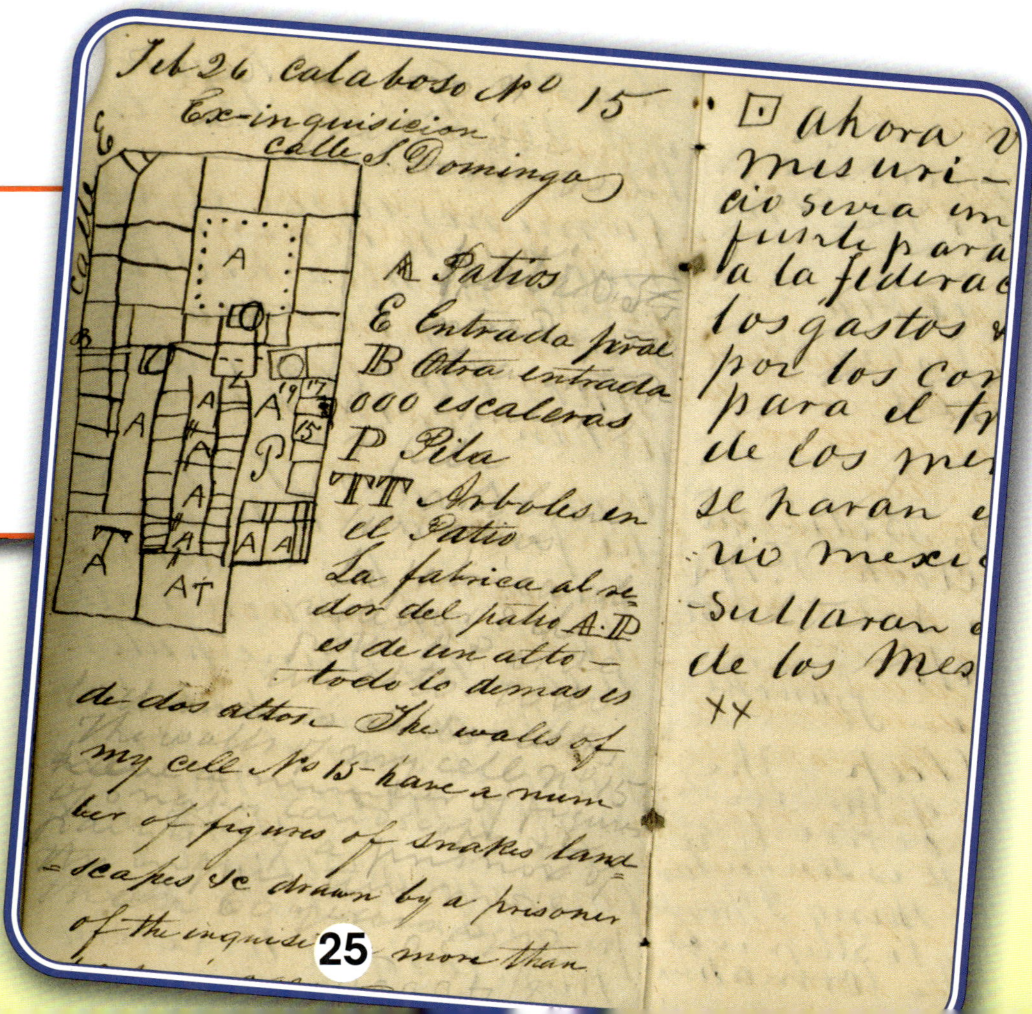

Stephen was locked in a prison cell for almost a year. This is a map he drew of his prison while he was there.

5 INDEPENDENCE!

On July 13, 1835, Stephen finally received permission to leave Mexico City. He sailed to New Orleans, Louisiana, where he worked toward "Americanizing Texas." Stephen wanted Texas to become part of the United States. He asked his cousin Mary to encourage more Anglo Americans to immigrate to Texas. He also hoped that Mexico would sell Texas to the United States willingly and peacefully.

WAR OR PEACE?

When Stephen finally returned to Texas in September 1835, he was given a warm welcome. He supported holding a convention, called the Consultation, to discuss the growing threat of war with Mexico and to form a local government for the people of Texas. A committee in San Felipe elected Stephen its chairman. While preparing for the Consultation, Stephen learned that the Mexican government was sending troops to stop any rebellion in Texas. Stephen ordered each district to organize a **militia**. Although there had been several small battles in earlier years, war officially began on October 1, 1835, with the Battle of Gonzales.

ARMY OF THE PEOPLE

On September 20, 500 Mexican troops, led by General Martín Perfecto de Cos, began marching toward San Antonio. Stephen was elected to command the newly formed militia, called the Army of the People, in October and marched them to San Antonio. When they arrived Stephen offered a peaceful settlement, but Cos refused.

► *General Martín Perfecto de Cos had personal ties with President Santa Anna. Cos was married to Santa Anna's sister.*

CONCEPCIÓN

On October 28, 1835, Cos's troops attacked about 100 men from the Army of the People at the Battle of Concepción. The Texans had a good defensive position and the Mexican soldiers attacked on open ground. More than 50 Mexican soldiers were killed and only one Texan died. Cos's men were forced to retreat to the fort.

The Consultation decided to form a temporary state government. The delegates chose an Anglo American named Sam Houston to command their army. They also chose to send Stephen and two other men, William Wharton and Branch Archer, to the United States to gather American support for Texas. The three commissioners left for the United States in late December of 1835. They successfully secured loans, more weapons and ships, and more soldiers for the cause.

After the Battle of Concepción in 1835, Sam Houston was elected commander of the Texas army.

TEXAS INDEPENDENCE

Meanwhile, several more battles were fought in early 1836, leading up to the final battle at San Jacinto on April 21, 1836. Sam Houston's men surprised Santa Anna's Mexican forces there. The battle lasted about 20 minutes. Many Mexican soldiers were killed or taken prisoner. The Texan army had fewer **casualties**, but Sam Houston had been shot and his ankle was shattered. The next day, Santa Anna was captured and taken prisoner. Texas had won its independence from Mexico.

CANDIDATE FOR PRESIDENT

Stephen learned about the Battle of San Jacinto and Santa Anna's capture when he returned to New Orleans in June. The newly independent nation of Texas was in need of its own system of government. Stephen announced his candidacy for president of Texas.

In a letter to the editor of the *Telegraph and Texas Register*, Stephen wrote:

> ***"...I came to Texas...to serve the country in any capacity in which the people might think proper to employ me, I shall not decline the highly responsible and difficult one now proposed, should the majority of my fellow citizens elect me."***

SECRETARY OF STATE

Stephen was expected to become the first president of Texas. However, the popular military leader Sam Houston announced his candidacy for president just 11 days before the **election**. Sam Houston won by a landslide. A few days after Sam Houston became president, he sent Stephen a letter in which he asked him to be the secretary of state for Texas. In Stephen's new position, he worked toward the goal of having the United States **annex** Texas. The winter after he took the job was very cold, and Stephen became very ill with pneumonia. On December 27, 1836, Stephen Austin died. It is said that his last words were, "The independence of Texas is recognized!"

This was Stephen's office and bedroom at Peach Point Plantation, where he died.

6 STEPHEN'S LEGACY

Stephen was only 43 years old when he died, but he had accomplished a great deal. Without Stephen's vision and determination, Texas, as it is known today, would not exist.

WORKS OF ART

Various paintings and sculptures of Stephen have been created since his death. Many are in government buildings in Texas. In his 1875 painting, called *The Settlement of Austin's Colony*, Henry McArdle showed Stephen with a rifle in one hand and a Texas land title in the other. The original painting is in the Texas State Capitol building in Austin, Texas.

On December 10, 1838, Stephen's friend and colleague, Mirabeau Lamar, succeeded Sam Houston as president of Texas. Lamar moved the capital of Texas to a new town named after Stephen. Today, Austin is still the capital of Texas.

PLACES OF HONOR

Many Texas schools are named after Stephen Austin. The oldest educational institution in Texas is Austin College, which was founded in 1849 in Sherman, Texas. The Stephen F. Austin State University, in Nacogdoches, Texas, is named after Stephen. Many high schools, middle schools, and elementary schools bear his name, too. Many people from around the world visit the Stephen F. Austin State Historical Park, in Austin County. The park, covering 667 acres (270 ha), is home to the original site of San Felipe de Austin, which Stephen founded.

Texas Perspective

When Texas's president, Sam Houston, learned of Stephen's death, he called Stephen the "Father of Texas."

LEARNING MORE

BOOKS

Haley, James L. *Stephen F. Austin and the Founding of Texas.* The Library of American Lives and Times. New York: Rosen Publishing, 2004.

Roberts, Russell. *The Life and Times of Stephen F. Austin.* Profiles in American History. Hockessin, DE: Mitchell Lane Publishers, 2008.

HISTORIC SITES

Stephen Austin State Historical Park
www.tpwd.state.tx.us/state-parks/stephen-f-austin

WEBSITES

Handbook of Texas Online—Moses Austin
www.tshaonline.org/handbook/online/articles/fau12

PBS—Stephen Austin
www.pbs.org/weta/thewest/people/a_c/austin.htm

San Felipe de Austin
www.visitsanfelipedeaustin.com/index.aspx?page=17

Texas State Historical Association
www.tshaonline.org/handbook/online/articles/fau14

TIMELINE

Texas | Stephen F. Austin

- **1793** Stephen Fuller Austin is born in Austinville, Virginia, on November 3.
- **1797** Moves to Louisiana territory with family.
- **1804** Attends Bacon Academy in Colchester, Connecticut, until 1807.
- **1808** Stephen attends Transylvania University in Lexington, Kentucky, until 1810.
- **1812** Helps father in lead mining business in Potosi, Missouri.
- **1813** Enlists in the militia during War of 1812.
- **1820** Works for lawyer Joseph H. Hawkins in New Orleans, Louisiana.
- **1821** Takes over father's land grant in Texas.
- **1823** Settles 300 families, called the Old Three Hundred, in Texas.
- **1824** Capital of Austin's colony founded in San Felipe de Austin.
- **1826** Joins with Mexican forces to stop the Fredonian Rebellion.
- **1830** Mexico passes new law that stops more Americans from settling in Texas.
- **1833** Serves as president of the Convention of 1833 and delivers colonists' petition to Mexican leaders.
- **1834** Imprisoned in Mexico City from January 2 to December 25.
- **1835** Returns to Texas on September 8.
- **1835** Mexican troops march to San Antonio, where skirmish breaks out on September 20; Texas Revolution begins; Battle of Gonzales occurs on October 1; Battle of Concepción takes place on October 28.
- **1836** Battle of the Alamo takes place on March 6; Battle of San Jacinto ends Texas Revolution.
- **1836** Runs for president of the Republic of Texas but loses to Sam Houston. Appointed secretary of state by President Houston.
- **1836** Stephen Austin dies in Columbia, Texas, on December 27, 1836.

GLOSSARY

advertisement (ad-vur-TYZ-ment) A public notice that tells people about a product, an event, or something a person needs.
annex (A-neks) To take over or add to.
casualties (KA-zhul-teez) People who are injured or killed in an accident or a war.
colony (KAH-luh-nee) A new place where people move that is still ruled by the leaders of the country from which they came.
debt (DET) Something owed.
delegate (DEH-lih-get) A representative elected to attend a political gathering.
election (ee-LEK-shun) Choosing someone for a position by voting for him or her.
empresario (em-pruh-SEHR-ee-oh) A general manager with broad powers and responsibilities.
governor (GUH-vun-ur) Someone elected as head of a state, or an official who is put in charge by a king or queen.
immigrating (IH-muh-grayt-ing) Moving to another country to live.
loyalist (LOY-uh-list) A person who is loyal to a certain political party, government, or ruler.
militia (muh-LIH-shuh) A group of people who are trained and ready to fight when needed.
petition (puh-TIH-shun) A formal way to ask for something to be done.
pioneer (py-uh-NEER) A person who starts or helps to open up new ideas or things in new places.
population (pop-yoo-LAY-shun) A group of animals or people living in the same area.
province (PRAH-vins) One of the main parts of a country.
regiment (REH-juh-ment) A group in the military.
revolution (reh-vuh-LOO-shun) A complete change in government.
War of 1812 (WOR UV AY-teen TWELV) A war between the United States and Britain, fought from 1812 to 1815.

INDEX